Cut the Check!

Successful Strategies for Increasing Donor Engagement and Fundraising

(1st Edition)

by:

Keith E. Cradle, Ph.D.

E-mail: mrcradle@yahoo.com

Web: http://www.keithcradle.com

Copyright © 2018 by Keith E. Cradle, Ph.D.

All rights reserved. No part of this book shall be reproduced or transmitted in any form or by any means, electronic, mechanical, magnetic, photographic including photocopying, recording or by any information storage and retrieval system, without prior written permission of the publisher. No patent liability is assumed with respect to the use of the information contained herein. Although every precaution has been taken in the preparation of this book, the publisher and author assume no responsibility for errors or omissions. Neither is any liability assumed for damages resulting from the use of the information contained herein.

ISBN: 978-1726359900

Published by:

Crafted with Cradle Publications

Crafted with Cradle, LLC.

Web: http://www.keithcradle.com

E-mail: mrcradle@yahoo.com

IG: @dr_cradle & @craftedwithcradle

Twitter: @dr_cradle

About the Author

Keith Cradle, Ph.D. is a community engagement specialist, cultural arts advocate and a nonprofit strategist with over 25 years of experience.

Dr. Cradle is currently on the Board of Directors for Carolina Voices (www.carolinavoices.org), The Bechtler Museum (www.bechtler.org), Inspire the Fire (www.inspirethefire.org) and the Juvenile Crime Prevention Council for Mecklenburg County. Keith's involvement and commitment to the development of the arts and cultural sectors of Charlotte have led him to help start the Jail Arts Project with the Bechtler Museum that works with youth in detention discover, develop and harness their appreciation for art.

His community-based initiatives have been awarded the 2001 NACO award for outstanding program of the year in the state of North Carolina, the Golden Project Award 2004 from the North Carolina Public Health Association, the Kathy Kerr Outstanding Health Education Project Award 2004, 2006 APPCNC Award for pregnancy prevention program of the year in North Carolina, and the 2007 Outstanding Service Award from Crossroads Charter High School [CMS]. In 2012, he was awarded the Young and Powerful for Obama Rising Star Award. He was previously selected into the Community Building Initiatives Leaders under 40 and Charlotte Style Magazines 75 Most Stylish.

He has a BA in Communications from Johnson C. Smith University, a Master's degree in Health Administration from the University of North Carolina at Charlotte, a MBA/MSL from Pfeiffer University in Charlotte, NC and his PhD in Organizational Leadership & Management from Walden University in Baltimore, MD.

Dedication

This book is dedicated to my family and friends that have stood by me through it all. To my mom and dad, thank you for the gift of life. I promise to never waste it. To my brother, thank you for everything. And I mean, everything. To my Ama, there are not enough words or acknowledgements available to properly put into context what you've meant to me and our family. It has been your ceaseless prayers that have moved this family through the years. My sister Monica, for being a friend and confidant. Finally, to my nieces Sydney and Logan, this book is dedicated to the boundless thoughts that you two can do anything and be anything.

Acknowledgements

I want to acknowledge my friends. Vince Alexander, through thick and through thin. Badboys for life. Rahjah, Taswell, T. Guess, Dylan, Jameka, Chuck, Eric, Tasha, Pangi, D Black, Damian, Jermaine, Jazz, Al Poconos, Mumz, Hester, Jennifer, Obas, Smoak, Vance, Sonya, Kwain, Adrian, Brooks [RIH] and Shorty, this book reflects the long days and even longer nights of conversation, insight and love you have all provided me.

To my Big Cousins; Foots, D-Dubbz, and Rusty, love you guys!

To my Line Brothers, the 9 Gods of Chaos, Alpha Omicron, Fall 1993, APHIA. Chris, Thomas [R.I.H.], Mark, Rich, Toure, Rick, Mel and Frank, it was the bond we created back at JCSU that has held me together all these years. Love you guys. And to my AO Chapter Bros, thank you!

To Ralph and Chance, my writing cohort. Thank you, Ralph for being my Pastor and friend. Your consistent comments and jokes were the push in the back to keep me writing and finishing. Chance, thank you brother for being the "Coach." You mapped out the plays and we executed to the best of our ability.

To my Johnson C. Smith University, UNCC, Pfeiffer and Walden University family, thank you for pushing me and challenging my educational goals. Each marker was a point in my life that was needed and necessary. Thank you.

To the city of White Plains, NY, I wrote this book because of you. It was from those streets, schools and experiences that I was forged and cultivated a curious desire to never settle. To always keep moving forward. To push harder. To not quit. Don't complain. And to never not work.

Finally, I acknowledge all the nonprofit organizations that wish to do well in their selective communities. I wrote this book so that it will help and assist with the mission and visions of your organizations. May you use its pages to further increase your donations and further your goals.

Table of Contents

About the Author	iii.
Dedication	v.
Acknowledgements	vi.
Foreword	xi.
Chapter 1: What is Donor Engagement?	1-25
Chapter 2: What is in the Ground?	26-43
Chapter 3: Pitch Perfect	44-54
Chapter 4: Staying Connected	55-60
Chapter 5: The Long View	61-71
Chapter 6: What's Next?	72-73
Appendix A: Sample Call Sheet	74
Appendix B: Sample Donor Email	76
References	78

"Challenges are what make us human, fighting off failure, showing people you are the best, that you've been preparing for this moment…" K. Irving

Foreword

The donation baskets were empty!

The fundraiser we planned for months was a fund LOSER! We sent invitations to potential donors to attend a catered lunch to learn about a new "Community Beautification Program" we wanted to offer the youth we served. Over 50 potential donors attended the lunch and enjoyed lasagna, garlic bread, salad, banana pudding, tea, and water. We made our "pitch" that included an itemized budget using an animated PowerPoint presentation while they ate.

We allowed them to finish their meal and then asked them for questions regarding the purpose and importance of allowing our youth to learn how to improve the appearance of their communities. We answered the questions, gave them envelopes to place their donations, and asked them to place the envelopes in the donation baskets by the exit doors with bright red balloons attached. When the lunch ended, we thanked everyone for coming and reminded the potential donors of the amount of money we needed and how it would be used to enhance the appearance of local communities. After everyone left, we retrieved the baskets and they were empty --- not one penny!! We were confused, angry, and frustrated. How could our fundraising efforts fail so badly? How could we tell the Board of Directors that the money they approved to host the fundraising event did not yield a return?

As the founder and executive director of Comprehensive Community Based Solutions, Incorporated, this fund loser really happened and was one of a few we experienced over the ten years we provided community services. The overall revenue generation strategies we used were haphazard at best. We struggled to retain reliable donors who made donations regularly, we did not have a dedicated grant writer to write grant proposals, and most of our fundraisers were fund losers. It seemed that we always struggled financially while offering excellent services for black male youth in our communities. Nevertheless, we were determined to continue working hard because we saw the positive impact our services had on the young men who received them.

One day we received a check from a foundation in which we had not requested funding. Shocked, confused, and grateful, we called the foundation to find out why we received the check. They told us that Keith Cradle, a Board Member, recommended the Emerging Leaders Mentorship Program for Black Male Youth to receive the grant funding. After getting his contact information, I called Keith to thank him and let him know how much we appreciated his recommendation and promised that the money would be invested wisely.

Since that first connection with Keith several years ago, we have watched his great work and deeds in the community. He serves on several boards of directors, hosts an informative Podcast (Crafted With Cradle), and is always willing to share his knowledge. In fact, Keith recently took time from his very busy schedule to facilitate a session on "Effective Board Development" for an event I hosted. His honest, authentic persona and genuine concern about the community makes him the perfect author of a book that helps nonprofit professionals learn how to sustain their services through effective fundraising strategies. Therefore, I am honored and humbled to write a foreword for his amazing book, "Cut the Check! Successful Strategies for Increasing Donor Engagement and Fundraising".

After reading the phenomenal book that Keith wrote, the mistakes we made with our first fund loser became evident. For example, we did not know anything about the steps required to develop donor engagement strategies or how to cultivate relationships with donors to enhance fundraising. "Cut the Check!: Successful Strategies for Increasing Donor Engagement and Fundraising" is a very easy book to read that seemingly takes you by the hand and walks you through the six chapters teaching you step-by-step how to create strategies to develop sustainable streams of revenue for your nonprofit organizations through donor engagement and effective fundraising strategies.

Specifically, this is the perfect book for nonprofit professionals who need a foundational approach to understanding the process of donor engagement, how community giving works, tips to "making the pitch", the process to following up after the pitch, and how to sustain the great services you are providing in the communities you serve.

Let's be honest, most nonprofit professionals are burning the candle at both ends trying to generate revenues, offer excellent programs and services for their clients, provide reports to the stakeholders and community members, and constantly put out fires. As a result, they do not spend as much time as they should be using resources (like books) that would make their jobs easier and the results more successful.

Take it from me, taking the time to read "Cut the Check!: Successful Strategies for Increasing Donor Engagement and Fundraising" written by my friend, Dr. Keith Cradle will help you turn your entire fundraising strategy around and your will see a return on your investments immediately after implementing the tools he shares.

Just a few things you will learn include what donor engagement means and how to implement traditional and non-traditional strategies; the differences between long-term and short-term donor engagements; how to incorporate social medial fundraising strategies; and how to reach out to millennials minority donors who are often overlooked.

Another important part of the "Cut the Check!: Successful Strategies for Increasing Donor Engagement and

Fundraising" book that would have helped our team tremendously is the way Dr. Cradle explains how to make the "elevator speech" when you are in the presence of a potential donor. Not only does he walk you through the process, he also teaches us four tips to use when making the "ask" for the donation.

Congratulations on your decision to purchase the "Cut the Check! Successful Strategies for Increasing Donor Engagement and Fundraising" book written by Dr. Keith Cradle. You made a wise investment. The book is very easy to read with step-by-step instructions. and key strategies at the end of each chapter.

In closing, Keith is an expert in the field of donor engagement and fundraising. His impeccable educational credentials, his service on boards of directors, his practical experience with donor engagement and fundraising, and his genuine desire to help nonprofit professionals sustain make him the perfect author for this type of book. It will not take long for you to realize that this book is an excellent choice for the development of your team and the enhancement of their donor engagement and fundraising skills.

Susan Woods, MBA, MAT

Founder of Comprehensive Community Based Solutions, Incorporated

Owner of LCM Educational Resources DBA Susan **Woods Nonprofit Solutions**

www.AskSusanWoods.com

Chapter 1: What is Donor Engagement?

Nonprofit agencies are instrumental in U.S. society and local communities. Development Directors are charged with seeking viable and sustainable streams of income. While there is significant outreach being done within organizations, there is always more work to be done. The purpose of this book is to explore successful strategies Development Directors can use to engage and increase donors. The focus of this book will outline the following key components: (a) working definition of donor engagement; (b) strategies of how to spot what is in the community landscape and; (c) success strategies on how to make winning engagement pitches. Research has shown in the past that community development, fostering relationships and intentional engagement are themes that attract most donors. The information presented in this book is socially significant because nonprofit leaders rely on a stable donor base, so they can positively impact the local community. By addressing engagement strategies with a significant portion of the community, nonprofit leaders can attract and retain donors for continued sustainability.

What is Donor Engagement?

Traditional vs. Non-Traditional

When Development Directors create engagement strategies they normally do so from a familiar schematic. The normal or traditional route is to solicit people that live in the community but have ties to wealth and influence. Development Directors have used many types of development strategies over the course of time. Fundraising is unique to every organization, but development professionals typically use many of the same platforms and frameworks regarding engagement and securing patrons (Brown & Guo, 2010). These strategies include but are not limited to direct mailers, target donor lists, marketing materials, and social media. Social media is the newest platform that many Development Directors are using to attract and engage younger donors. By posting images and phrases that identify the good works of the organization, potential donors can see where their resources go. Per Kirk et al. (2016), social media is the least expensive of current development strategies and can have a wider reach given its global platform.

Nonprofit development strategies also push into nontraditional areas, such as allowing donors to dictate where and how they want their gifts used. Giving donors control over the use of the funds or in-kind donation increases the motivation to donate (Khodakarami, Petersen, & Venkatesan, 2015). Patrons who have an increased involvement and interest participate more.

This increased involvement can also spill over into how Development Directors or those responsible for generating funds target their base. Organizations that have the resources are using software and studies to determine what areas or concerns are important to donors. This process allows Development Directors to spotlight areas donors are offering the most money (Waniak-Michalak & Zarzycka, 2015). By mining financial information, Development Directors can construct a more detailed approach for selecting donors in their community.

Along with selecting donors in their community, celebrity endorsements or capitalizing on celebrity branding can increase donations to a nonprofit organization. Celebrities have a certain sway on the public, and the perception that they are giving to a specific cause will move others to do the same. High visibility for a nonprofit and a cause is a development strategy that can boost awareness and donations (Ilicic & Baxter, 2014). However, the use of celebrities is not a proven tactic to increase long-term engagement for committed and engaged donors.

Fundraising efforts are also starting to become convoluted due to priority strategies placed on donors. Boenigk and Scherhag (2014) studied the effects of nonprofit organizations prioritizing donors based on giving levels and donor loyalty. Some of the data showed that groups not placed in high regard left for other institutions. This lack of regard leads to disengagement due to dissatisfaction or bad community relationships (Boenigk & Scherhag, 2014). Additionally, there can be disengagement from donor strategy if it does speak clearly to all stakeholders (Scherhag & Boenigk, 2013). Because of the lack of intentional engagement, Development Directors usually leave minorities out of the traditional tiered-priority strategy that utilizes several price or entry points to membership or donating.

Competition has increased between nonprofits for donations and other resources. This competition stems from an increase in the number of available nonprofit organizations people can choose from (Grizzle, 2015). Nonprofit leaders that demonstrate a credible and viable development strategy likely attract a higher number of donations (Grizzle, 2015). Calabrese and Grizzle (2012) outlined the continued importance of Development Directors engaging nontraditional groups and appealing to local interests when creating a development strategy.

Nonprofit leaders similarly deal with the expectation of creating trust and commitment in donors. Building a sustainable base of donors involves long-term effectiveness (Powers & Yaros, 2012). Powers and Yaros (2012) highlighted the efforts made to make inroads into neighborhoods using open forums meant to cultivate support through honest dialogue. Communities that feel as though they are a part of any process, especially fundraising campaigns, tend to vest and collaborate more in the strategy. Open forums are a good portal for including stakeholders and longtime residents in discussions that hopefully will help their community.

The continued challenges for nonprofit leaders to attract donors extend from strategic planning to volunteer relationships. Volunteer partnerships are often neglected, but have the potential to provide huge value to a nonprofit's development strategy (Samuel, Wolf, & Schilling, 2013). Building a competitive advantage in the nonprofit sector can begin with a word-of-mouth strategy and positive verbal contributions from volunteers (Schloderer, Sarstedt, & Ringle, 2014). Addressing engagement can begin with the daily interactions of staff, volunteers, and the targeted community.

Why Organizations Need to Engage and Fundraise

Charitable giving is a choice and the amount given changes over time (Mataira, Morelli, Matsuoka & Uehara-McDonald, 2014). This fundamental concept also underscores the amount that people give and where they give (Gasman, 2010). The extensive choices associated with donor involvement and development can create challenges for staff members who are responsible for procuring long-term donations (Mataira et al., 2014). The more choices potential donors have the more offsetting it can be to attempt to procure funds from them. This assumed hinderance could lead to strategic mismanagement or a lessened focus on nontraditional potential donors.

The U.S. economy has been in flux since 2008, with some considerable rebound in recent years. Fundraisers and nonprofit organization leaders have recognized that individual donors are giving less or only giving to select organizations. Ford and Merchant (2010) discussed the decreasing amounts by donors and the decreasing number of donors. Individual donors continue to represent the largest source of revenue for nonprofits (Ko, Gibson, & Kim, 2011).

Considering these factors, long-term and sustainable involvement for donors with one nonprofit is becoming harder (Cacija, 2014). Donor cultivation and donor engagement are vital functions of a nonprofit organization's long-term sustainability. Nonprofit organizational leaders across a broad spectrum are consistently looking for ways to expand donor bases and build capacity (Millar & Doherty, 2016). Technology has also affected the way donors engage as well as how they use their resources (Kirk, Abrahams, & Ractham, 2016).

Understanding and examining factors contributing to successful engagement with donors is an ongoing exercise. All nonprofit organizations hope to engage donors in ways that increase their charitable giving. There is a plethora of literature showing how nonprofit leaders have improved fundraising efforts toward sustainability. Fundraising has basic tenets that all start with a developmental plan (Aaker & Mogilner, 2010).

Development personnel of small and medium-sized nonprofits must fundraise vigorously with fewer resources, which leads to creative and nontraditional fundraising mediums (Schneider, 2003).

Long Term vs Short Term Engagement

The amount of time an organization desires for engagement depends on the organizations needs and perceived sustainability. Engaging with donors or potential donors can be for short periods of time or longer but the end results can be vastly different. Organizations should examine their donor structure along with their capacity, scope and scale to decide which engagement term works best for them.

When it comes to scope and scale, every organization will approach it differently. The length and breadth of the campaign is the scope. How narrow or wide do you want to cast your nets? The scale is the amount of people you are looking to target. You can essentially do a narrow campaign [which looks at a certain number of neighborhoods or businesses] but is targeting everyone that lives or works there. Conversely, an organization can have a wide scale city approach but only want women of a certain age. By defining the variables early in the planning, engaging donors becomes more intentional.

Long term engagement is typically the route most development directors and organizations choose. Short term engagement is normally rolled out when there is not a lot of time or commitment energy from older or newer donors. Both engagement strategies consist of potential donor identification, theorized engagement strategies, realized engagement [actual activities] and timed follow-up.

- In the identification phase, Development Directors or staff are looking at the landscape and locating possible new and expired donors. If it is possible, you should look for previous records of expired donors to see what they have contributed in the past so that when the ask is made, it lines up to what the donor is used to.

- The second phase of long or short-term engagement is strategizing. In this portion, the team is creating or thinking of ways to logically engage all potential donors. Usually, there is a generalized strategy for all members but this is where an organization can mix it up and create individualized plans for select members or groups.
- Actual engagement or realized engagement is when the plan is placed into action. The strategy that was chosen becomes the medium for reaching out to the public. It is also in this phase that staff should begin the process of collecting data for outcomes/processes to see what is working or not working.

- Finally, the last phase is timed follow-up. Once the campaign is completed, there should be follow up with all that were contacted. This allows for more feedback plus gives new donors continued connectivity as they navigate their giving or membership. It is also here that the collected data comes in handy for engagement adjustments.

Following these steps allows for a practical plan of implementation and coordination. Development Directors should make the right determinant for how long they plan to engage potential new donors given their capacity. Spending a lot of time or resources on a few potential donors during a long-term engagement strategy may not be the best use of time. However, a short-term strategy may not be enough time to persuade potential donors of the benefits of aligning with your organizational cause.

Social Media and Engagement

Fundraising and engagement strategies are shifting to technological mediums. Social networking sites are valuable tools for stakeholder and donor engagement (Ihm, 2015). Courting new donors will increasingly take place through the technological and social platforms that are of interest to them (Ihm, 2015). Swanson (2013) noted that organizational leaders who blend technology with an organization's social capital fare better in long-term development.

Examples of social media use exist on platforms such as Twitter, Facebook, Snapchat, and Instagram. Nonprofit institutions are typically early adopters of current technology (Smitko, 2012). Lovejoy, Waters, and Saxton (2012) noted that having multiple ways to learn about the organization can develop or strengthen donor relationships. Engaged institutions have short- and long-term development strategies that might help to address communication issues with donors (Swanson, 2013).

The level of public engagement on social media differs between organizations. However, institutional leaders must be cognizant of the value that social media platforms bring (Cho, Schweickart, & Haase, 2014). Mano (2014) contended that social media, and the networking attached to it, gathers together people of like-minded interests. This similar thinking affects their giving behavior. As societal demographics change, giving strategies must also change to attract diverse donor bases (Mano, 2014).

Social networking sites are also a platform for gaining traction with younger donors. The next generation of donors, and particularly African Americans, are looking to platforms that make giving easier (Mottino & Miller, 2005). However, many nonprofit organizations do not court minorities specifically but instead choose to create generic engagement strategies that encompass just volunteering (Kim & Lee, 2014). This level of engagement attracts some donors, but not many, as the strategy is not holistic and does not intersect with social and technological trends (Mottino & Miller, 2005).

Consistent innovation in the workplace and with organizational leaders creates an environment for success and is vital to a nonprofit organization's survival and long-term sustainability (McMurray, Islam, Sarros, & Pirola-Merlo, 2013). Nonprofit executives cultivate and nurture innovation at the leadership level, and it becomes part of the organizational culture (Chapleo, 2015). However, nonprofit leaders must communicate these ideals effectively.

Key Questions Organizations Should Ask in Route to Increased Engagement

1. Why is donor engagement important to your organization?
2. What are our current engagement strategies? Are they working?
3. What tools do we have at our disposal to increase awareness and engagement?

Key Strategies for Increasing Engagement

1. Clearly communicate with responsible staff why engagement is vital. Show them examples of strategies that are successful. Produce the financial statements and breakdown the amount of funding that is donor supplied.
2. Discuss the differences between short-term engagement strategies vs long-term engagement strategies. Then breakdown what your potential donors respond to better.
3. Assess what tools your organization is functional in and can use to increase engagement.

References

Aaker, J. V., & Mogilner, C. (2010). Nonprofits are seen as warm and for-profits as competent: Firm stereotypes matter. *Journal of Consumer, 37,* 224-237. doi:10.1086/651566

Boenigk, S., & Scherhag, C. (2014). Effects of donor priority strategy on relationship fundraising outcomes. *Nonprofit Management & Leadership, 24,* 307-336. doi:10.1002/nml.21092

Brown, G., & Guo, C. (2010). Exploring the key roles for nonprofit boards. *Nonprofit and Voluntary Sector Quarterly, 39,* 536-546. Retrieved from http://journals.sagepub.com/home/nvs

Cacija, N. (2014). Preliminary empirical analysis of the relationship dynamics between marketing activities and fundraising success in nonprofit organizations.

Management Journal of Contemporary Management, 19, 137-155. Retrieved from https://moj.efst.hr/management/

Calabrese, T., & Grizzle, C. (2012). Debt, donors, and the decision to give. *Journal of Pubic Budgeting, Accounting and Financial Management, 24*, 221-254. Retrieved from http://pracademics.com/index.php/jpbafm

Chapleo, C. (2015). Brand "infrastructure" in nonprofit organizations: Challenges to successful brand building? *Journal of Marketing Communications, 21*, 199-209. doi:10.1080/13527266.2012.741609

Cho, M., Schweickart, T., & Haase, A. (2014). Public engagement with nonprofit organizations on Facebook. *Public Relations Review, 40*, 565-567. doi:10.1016/j.pubrev.2014.01.008

Ford, J. B., & Merchant, A. (2010). Nostalgia drives donations: The power of charitable appeals based on emotions and intentions. *Journal of Advertising Research, 50,* 450. doi:10.2501/S0021849910091592

Gasman, M. (2010). A growing tradition? *Nonprofit Management and Leadership, 21,* 121-138. doi:10.1002/nml.20016

Grizzle, C. (2015). Efficiency, stability and the decision to give to nonprofit arts and cultural organizations in the United States. *International Journal of Nonprofit and Voluntary Sector Marketing, 20,* 226-237. doi:10.1002/nvsm.1521

Ihm, J. (2015). Network measures to evaluate stakeholder engagement with nonprofit organizations on social networking sites. *Public Relations Review, 41,* 501-503. doi:10.1016/j.pubrev.2015.06.018

Ilicic, J., & Baxter, S. (2014). Fit in celebrity-charity alliances: When perceived celanthropy benefits nonprofit organisations. *International Journal of Nonprofit and Voluntary Sector Marketing, 16,* 200-208. doi:10.1002/nvsm.1497

Khodakarami, F., Petersen, J., & Venkatesan, R. (2015). Developing donor relationships:

The role of the breadth of giving. *Journal of Marketing, 79,* 77-93.

doi:10.1509/jm.14.0351

Kim, Y., & Lee, W. (2014). Networking for philanthropy: Increasing volunteer behavior via social networking sites. *Cyberpsychology, Behavior, and Social Networking,*

17(3), 160-165. doi:10.1089/cyber.2012.0415

Kirk, K., Abrahams, A., & Ractham, P. (2016). E-progression of nonprofit organization websites: US versus Thai charities. *Journal of Computer Information Systems, 56,*

244-252. doi:10.1080.08874417.2016.153918

Ko, Y. J., Gibson, H., & Kim, M. (2011). Understanding donors: A case of university performing arts programs in the USA. *International Journal of Nonprofit and Voluntary Sector Marketing, 16*, 166-182. doi:10.1002/nvsm.411

Lovejoy, K., Waters, R., & Saxton, G. (2012). Engaging stakeholders through Twitter: How nonprofit organizations are getting more out of 140 characters or less. *Public Relations Review, 38*, 313-318. doi:10.1016/j.pubrev.2012.01.005

Mataira, P., Morelli, P., Matsuoka, J., & Uehara-McDonald, S. (2014). Shifting the paradigm: New directions for non-profits and funders in an era of diminishing resources. *Social Business, 4*, 231-244. doi:10.1362/204440814X14103454934212

Mano, R. (2014). Social media, social causes, giving behavior and money contributions.

Computers in Human Behavior, 31, 278-293. doi:10.1016/j.chb.2013.10.044

McMurray, A., Islam, M., Sarros, J., & Pirola-Merlo, A. (2013). Workplace innovation in a nonprofit organization. *Nonprofit Management & Leadership, 23,* 367-388. doi:10.1002/nml.21066

Millar, P., & Doherty, A. (2016). Capacity building in nonprofit sport organizations: Development of a process model. *Sport Management Review, 19,* 365-377. doi:10.1016/j.smr.2016.01.002

Mottino, F., & Miller, E. (2005). Philanthropy among African American donors in the New York metropolitan region: A generational analysis. *New Directions for Philanthropic Fundraising, 48,* 31-46. Retrieved from https://www.researchgate.net/journal/1542-7846_New_Directions_for_Philanthropic_Fundraising

Powers, E., & Yaros, R. (2012). Cultivating support for nonprofit news organizations:

> Commitment, trust, and donating audiences. *Journal of Communication*

Management, 17, 157-170. doi:10.1108/13632541311318756

Samuel, O., Wolf, P., & Schilling, A. (2013). Corporate

> volunteering: Benefits and challenges for

> nonprofits. *Nonprofit Management & Leadership, 24*, 163-179. doi:10.1002/nml.21089

Scherhag, C., & Boenigk, S. (2013). Different or equal

> treatment? Donor priority strategy and fundraising

> performance assessed by a propensity score

> matching study.

Nonprofit Management & Leadership, 23, 443-472. doi:10.1002/nml.21074

Schloderer, M., Sarstedt, M., & Ringle, C. (2014). The

> relevance of reputation in the nonprofit sector: The

> moderating effect of socio-demographic

> characteristics.

International Journal of Nonprofit and Voluntary Sector Marketing, 19, 110-126. doi:10.1002/nvsm.1491

Schneider, J. (2003). Small, minority-based nonprofits in the information age. *Nonprofit Management & Leadership, 13,* 385-399. doi:10.1002/nml.6

Smitko, K. (2012). Donor engagement through twitter. *Public Relations Review, 38,* 633-635. doi:10.1016/j.pubrev.2012.05.012

Swanson, L. (2013). A strategic framework for nonprofits. *Nonprofit Management & Leadership, 23,* 303-323. doi:10.1002/nml.21067

Waniak-Michalak, H., & Zarzycka, E. (2015). Financial and non-financial factors motivating individual donors to support public benefit organizations. *Comparative Economic Research, 18,* 131-152. doi:10.1515/cer-2015-0008

Chapter 2: What is in the Ground?

What does your giving community look like?

Once you've determined the engagement route you wish to take, the next step is analysis for cultivation. The community you live, work and recreate in has clues to what the giving community looks like. Development Directors can look on the websites of local organizations and see who is giving money to those organizations. Additionally, take ride around your community and look at your developing areas in town. The more developed the area, especially when it comes to arts/culture, the more resources are being poured into it.

Your giving community should be a representation of all those that live in the community. However, at times that may not be the case. This can be due to lack of engagement by Development Directors to various parts of the community. Central to any development strategy is the communication of the strategy. The person in charge of communication at a nonprofit organization should have solid relationships with the surrounding community and should diversify those efforts (Zhu & Cheung, 2014).

Nonprofit health organizations have been on the frontline of communication development strategies that tie into donor engagement and cultivation for years. McKeever (2013) discussed the various ways leaders of successful health organizations attracted donor funding by channeling and creating broad social messages. Diverse efforts are emerging with staffing as well as with targeted engagement and development efforts (Bortree & Waters, 2014). Leaders of organizations built on service to the community must design diverse strategies to engage and nurture what is in the communal ground.

Growing vs. Stagnant Philanthropic Environment

One of the primary assessments after assessing what is the ground for your community, is making a determinant to shifts and trends in the philanthropic environment. With all markets, you must determine if your market is growing or plateauing. This can be done by looking at shifts in giving and how donors are deciding to give over time periods. You can find shifts and trends by looking at IRS filings of nonprofits in your area. These filings show the amount of revenue generated by donations.

A growing market is easier to navigate and is helped by the cause, organization or product soliciting funds. Initial engagement is created by experiences and outreach to anyone that comes in contact with the organization. The donors in the growing market have discretionary funds and are willing to give freely. However, these same donors are going to be in the lists of every Development Director in your city. It is important to gauge their interests and play to those strengths.

The stagnant environment is harder to move through given solicitation efforts are going to be minimal. Many donors in this threshold are only giving to causes they have familiarity with or have been vested in for long periods of time. Engagement efforts for this group must be done in a more personable fashion with invitations to include face time with higher ups. Additionally, a stagnant market is the perfect time to set up engagement efforts for future donations. The donor may not agree to give right now but they are being cultivated for a later payoff.

Millennial and Younger Donors

The motivation for giving and the ways it relates to younger donors are vital for nonprofit organization leaders to understand. The motives for younger donors who fit in the millennial category could vary from older donors.

Whereas older donors receive the glut of any engagement strategy, the next generation of donors needs to be involved as well.

Younger candidates in the millennial category will be the foundation for the next generation of philanthropists. The birthdates for millennials range from 1980 to 2000 (Paulin, Ferguson, Schattke, & Jost, 2014). Millennials represent about 30% of the current population in America, and others should not overlook their presence (Paulin, Ferguson, Jost, & Fallu, 2014).

The process or processes for sustained engagement for millennials do not yet have full definitions. Along those lines are the perceived differences between Caucasian millennials and African American millennials. Given the historic context of African American charitable giving, Jackson (2001) highlighted that traditional giving and the shifting of those giving practices are vastly different from other racial and ethnic groups. Nonprofit leaders should be considering the factors that drive giving and then dig deeper to engage the next group of age-appropriate donors (Jackson, 2001).

Engagement for millennials has been generally directed at social media marketing campaigns. Social media has the power and influence to build a larger donor base given its technological reach. However, many organizations employ older adults that have no real expertise or prowess when it comes to creating engagement strategies for millennials. This same deficiency extends to the lack of creation for targeted efforts to attract minority millennials (Bucic, Harris, & Arli, 2012).

Nonprofit leaders should begin to invest heavily in social media marketing toward millennials given the wealth transfer that will occur over the next two decades. The transfer of wealth that many baby boomers will undergo as they get their end-of-life affairs in order is going to happen. Adult children or grandchildren will receive this wealth or resource allotment. The grandchildren or millennial generation will have decision-making power on where to donate funds.

Social media and nontraditional giving campaigns reach millennials. Organizational leaders who make inroads or connections to millennials will be at the forefront of creating a substantial donor base. Millennials, regardless of race, also want to see change and be a part of the change that nonprofits can achieve. Being a part of that change process means being involved with nonprofit organizations and increasing engagement. Nonprofit organization leaders develop strategies around engagement but neglect communication strategies targeted to their audience (Kim & Lee, 2014). As it pertains to younger candidates, there is a feeling that Development Directors do not reach out to them but expect donations and volunteerism (Jackson, 2001).

I suggest that nonprofit organizational leaders should forecast impending economic and cultural changes. By being in step with trends and shifts, organizational leaders can begin to attract and retain newer or neglected donor bases for future funding. Nonprofits leaders or Development Directors that have a focused strategy and engagement plan for potential younger donors will create connectivity and greater involvement with that organization.

Minority Donors

Development Directors must also design these messages with both race and age in mind. African Americans do not have one collective motivation to give based on race. Efforts to engage younger African Americans must take on the social concerns of the times (Jackson, 2001). Jackson (2001) highlights conscious frameworks in which younger African Americans like to be engaged. Examples of those engagement efforts include relevance to the African American community and connectivity to their career aspirations.

Nonprofit organizational leaders should seek to understand why African Americans give and what their key motivators are. This level of understanding can help create successful development strategies and giving campaigns (Carter & Marx, 2007). Historically, African Americans did not have a lot of wealth, but they understood community development and educational needs (Mottino & Miller, 2005). Using segmented information to create a donor campaign for a selected audience is not new. However, African Americans are still an "untapped philanthropic resource" given agencies are not engaging them effectively enough (Van Slyke et al., 2007).

Corporate Fundraising

Many nonprofit organizational leaders subscribe to using tools created for the for-profit sector when it comes to communication, public relations, and marketing strategies (Van Slyke et al., 2007). It would make sense to co-opt practices from for-profit companies that have been widely successful. Additionally, these methods are easily accessible and at times offered at a low cost, which allows nonprofit organizational leaders to capitalize on continued use. Despite the factors that would push a nonprofit leader or Development Director to use these fundraising tactics, many for-profit methodologies do not always incorporate nonprofit ideals. As noted earlier, the typical nonprofit donor has a certain motivation for giving and does not look for direct or instant impact upon donating (Malhotra & Smith, 2011). For-profit business strategies do not focus on the ethereal qualities of the nonprofit donor.

The fundraising approach can take on for-profit approaches but should include operational needs and analytical approaches to maximize success. With the wide range of choices patrons have, it can become increasing difficult for donors to select a nonprofit to which they would like to donate. Development Directors must make their organizations stand out or provide information to corporate donors that builds identification (Smith, Windmeijer, & Wright, 2013). Bentley (2014) studied and highlighted donor motivation. Bentley's findings pinpointed self-interest, altruism, and mixed motives as the top three types of donor motivation. Development Directors who have not had training in donor motivation will miss these prompts and find fundraising laborious and difficult (Bentley, 2014).

Identification for a nonprofit can make the difference in how much corporations donate or if they donate at all. The nonprofit market continues to grow and become crowded with causes the larger community care about. Development Directors must learn to leverage their brand as it relates to both fundraising and development strategies. Corporate donors engaged and cultivated through similar experiences that the nonprofit supports usually remain for longer periods. Corporations who make consistent contributions to an organization are valuable to the nonprofit and receive the organization's attention throughout the year. As nonprofits are not alike, they set their terms for levels of giving and annual goals. The mission and vision of nonprofits help determine the amount of fundraising needed each year.

To increase fundraising and create brand recognition, nonprofit leaders are turning to professional fundraising services or social enterprise. These services provide consultants to develop impact strategies that can increase donations or donor involvement (Wang, Duan, & Yu, 2016). However, small and medium-sized nonprofits that are community driven and understand local issues can create that same awareness by using grassroots platforms to attract corporate donors.

Key Questions

1. Is your giving community growing or stagnant?
2. Who are the primary stakeholders in your community?
3. What are the primary interests of the stakeholders in your community?

Recommendations for Engaging Community Stakeholders

1. Discover and unlock donor motivation. Self-interest, altruism, and mixed motives are the top three types of donor motivation. When possible, make sure to send individualized notes/correspondence to potential donors. Make the potential donors feel special.
2. Training in donor motivation for Development Directors. Practice makes better! The more training people go through,

the more comfortable they get with engaging potential donors and understanding how to move them from potential to actual donors.

3. Make fundraising fun and interesting. Throw events that keep the guest on their toes. Make sure they see where potential dollars will be funded and utilize performance based activities.

References

Bentley, J. (2014). Best practices in noncommercial radio fundraising: A practitioner perspective. *International Journal of Nonprofit and Voluntary Sector Marketing, 19,* 250-261. doi:10.1002/nvsm.1505

Bortree, D., & Waters, R. (2014). Race and inclusion in volunteerism: Using communication theory to improve volunteer retention. *Journal of Public Relations Research, 26,* 215-234. doi:10.1080/1062726X.2013.864245

Bucic, T., Harris, J., & Arli, D. (2012). Ethical consumers among the millennials: A cross national study. *Journal of Business Ethics, 110,* 113-131. Retrieved from https://www.jstor.org/journal/jbusiethi

Carter, V., & Marx, J. (2007). What motivates African-American charitable giving: Findings from a national sample. *Administration in Social Work, 31,* 67-85. doi:10.1300/J147v31n01_05

Jackson, T. (2001). Young African Americans: A new generation of giving behavior. *International Journal of Nonprofit and Voluntary Sector Marketing, 6,* 243-253.

Kim, Y., & Lee, W. (2014). Networking for philanthropy: Increasing volunteer behavior via social networking sites. *Cyberpsychology, Behavior, and Social Networking,*

17(3), 160-165. doi:10.1089/cyber.2012.0415

Malhotra, N., & Smith, A. (2011). Social and tax implications of planned giving. *Journal of Applied Business Research, 27,* 39-43. doi:10.19030/jabr.v27i6.6464

McKeever, B. (2013). From awareness to advocacy: Understanding nonprofit communication, participation, and support. *Journal of Public Relations Research,*

25, 307-328. doi:10.1080/1062726X.2013.806868

Mottino, F., & Miller, E. (2005). Philanthropy among African American donors in the

New York metropolitan region: A generational analysis. *New Directions for Philanthropic Fundraising, 48,* 31-46. Retrieved from https://www.researchgate.net/journal/1542-7846_New_Directions_for_Philanthropic_Fundraising

Paulin, M., Ferguson, R., Schattke, K., & Jost, N. (2014). Millennials, social media, prosocial emotions, and charitable causes: The paradox of gender differences. *Journal of Nonprofit & Public Sector Marketing, 26,* 335-353. doi:10.1080/104955142.2014.965069

Paulin, M., Ferguson, R., Jost, N., & Fallu, J. (2014). Motivating millennials to engage in charitable causes through social media. *Journal of Service Management, 25,* 334-348. doi:10.1108/JOSM-05-2013-0122

Smith, S., Windmeijer, F., & Wright, E. (2013). Peer effects in charitable giving: Evidence from the (running) field. *Economic Journal, 125,* 1053-1071. doi:10.1111/ecoj.12114

Van Slyke, D., Ashley, S., & Johnson, J. (2007). Nonprofit performance, fund-raising effectiveness, and strategies for engaging African Americans in philanthropy. *American Review of Public Administration, 37*, 278-305. doi:10.1177/0275074006294390

Wang, C., Duan, Z., & Yu, L. (2016). From nonprofit organization to social enterprise. *International Journal of Contemporary Hospitality Management, 28*, 1287-1306. doi:10.1108/IJCHM-05-2014-0230

Zhu, W., & Cheung, M. (2014). Multiple relationship-management roles among communicators in not-for-profit organizations. *Human Service Organizations: Management, Leadership & Governance, 38*, 423-434. doi:10.1080/23303131.2014.943918

Chapter 3: Pitch Perfect

Making the Pitch

When approaching corporations or individuals to donate to your organization, it is very important to have a pitch or elevator speech. By having a predetermined script, it makes it easier to engage and convey the purpose of the ask. A very good pitch captures the intended audience and envelopes them in an engaging manner. This short outline gives anyone listening the onus of wanting to learn more about the organization.

Attentive Development Directors understand that it takes time to nurture and fashion great relationships that produce sustainable asks. However, there will be times that an opportunity arises and a short pitch is needed. Having time or not, there should be an available script for the inevitable "ask."

The Opening

A good Development Director or board member should be able to explain the organization in 30 seconds or less. Trying to tell everything about the organization will consume a lot of time plus overwhelm the potential donor. Two to three sentences are all should be needed to sum up mission, vision and values of the organization.

The Ask

No one donor is the same, so that will entail various ways you will need to make an ask. However, with the right preparation and a consistent message, seeking out funding can get easier. During this portion of the process, it is very important to be direct and targeted with the ask. So here are some tips to get what you want.

1. *Know Thy Donor*

Whenever an organization or Development Director is going to approach someone for donations, it is vital that they know who exactly they are asking. You will need to know more than just their full government name or address. The more you know about a prospective donor, the better off you will be. Here are some of the details you should cultivate about your donor prior to the ask.

- Interests
- Estimated Income
- Prior Giving History
- Age

These fundamental insights on your prospective donor give your more cache when deciding to make an approach for donations.

2. *Know Thy Ask*

Nonprofit leaders and Development Directors should know exactly how much they are attempting to raise and for what causes they are raising the money for. Donors do not like ambiguity nor do they always want to make the choice of how much they should give you with a blank request. The best asks involve the following:

- Being direct
- Utilizing as much specificity as possible
- Giving the amount you want the donor to contribute

By taking a lot of the guess work out of the potential donor's hands, you stand a better chance at landing that donation.

3. *Know Thy Self*

Once you know the amount you want to ask for, you should be able to effectively communicate the mission, vision and values of the organization or cause. Potential donors attach themselves to messages or stories that resonate with their personal lives. Everyone is asking for money but that should not be the sole focus. Potential donors or members want more. They want to hear success stories, major accomplishments or outcomes that show how and where the money is being used.

- Details about events or fundraisers that had impact in the community
- Stories of the organization and its ties to service
- Positive outcomes [anecdotal/numerical] to highlight engagement
- Discuss the added value donors bring by attaching to your mission

Storytelling is very important when attempting to convince donors to give you their resources. Additionally, the process of creating indelible memories should start and end with previous supporters and results.

4. *Know Thy Lane*

Knowing what works and what does not is just as important as knowing your donor base. Looking back over fundraising strategies to see how well they performed is vital. You never want to roll out a scheme that had minimal effect but huge resource allotments. If you are not using a metric based software or system, it would be a good idea to look at one. Keeping track of your donors and what engagements work best for them helps with strategy improvement and cuts down on time consuming plans that may not work.

- Email
- Mobile apps for giving
- Social Engagement Sessions
- Direct Mailers

Once the decision is made to roll out the appropriate strategy, it is crucial to track and measure how those strategies work. This will determine if you need to revisit the idea later or scrap it all together.

Have a Script

Asking for donations or volunteers can be scary task for the uninitiated. Many people freeze up at the mere mention of having to cold call or sit down with a stranger and end the conversation with an ask for money. Whether in person or via some other communicative medium, you want to be as prepared as possible to get through the presentation. By developing a pre-made script, you can alleviate the burden or anxiety of coming up with talking points on the fly. The script does not have to be read word for word or memorized but does allow the comfort of having touch points throughout the conversation.

- Always introduce yourself, the organization and the role you play
- Ask a warm up question
- Give more information about the organization and why you are engaging
- Make the ask
- Let them know how their funds will be utilized

- Thank them for their time

A good script incorporates these touch points. It can be short or long but you want to make sure you are making the prospective donor feel welcome and not rushed to make decisions. Additionally, always think of the audience and who you are engaging. A younger donor may not have the same amount of time an older donor has or vice-versa. Try to be as individualized as possible.

ABC [Always Be Closing]

While it does not make for good grammar, the quintessential point for charting the end of the engagement conversation is to end with a result. Subsequently, that may not mean an ask that ends with a dollar amount. Closing the right way is just as paramount as closing the wrong way. Even if you do not end with the intended result, closing also means keeping the conversation open for another time.

Engagement is about creating and nurturing relationships. If the contact strategy does not net dollars, it can still capture a new friend. You want to ensure that conversation has progressed and moved your relationship a step further with the possibility of gaining a donation. A good Development Director [or the person doing the ask] should be utilizing these points to get a good close.

- Make sure the potential donor and yourself are on the same wave
- Let them know you are listening, hear them and any potential concerns/questions they may have
- Be understanding to their circumstances
- Guide the conversation towards an appropriate conclusion

The best closers and the utilization of ABC are those that understand what they are trying to accomplish. The ask and the pitch they are making is not phony but rooted in a connection to the person they are engaging. This engagement is an opportunity to tell the story not necessarily sell anything. At the end of the conversation, the close keeps the potential donor engaged and active with the organization, even if they do not contribute financial assistance at that time.

Key Questions Organizations Should Be Able to Answer

1. How much you are going to ask for?
2. What is your cause? What's the mission? Why are you asking?
3. What has worked or has not worked in the past?

Recommendations for the Proper Pitch

- Set the groundwork by knowing who and what you are asking for. You should know the audience you are addressing and what your donors like to hear. Additionally, you should be walking in with a set amount that you will be asking for.

- Educate, empower and inspire donors through story-telling. Make the stories personal. It's best if you have statements, videos or the actual person at the event to tell their story of success.
- Provide metrics or outcomes to drive the point home. The proof is in the pudding. Have short notes or easily readable cards that highlight metrics and successful outcomes you can pass out or leave around the room.

Chapter 4: Staying Connected

The Follow Up

After you have created the pitch and made the ask, dollars should be rolling in. Or not. However, the plan of action was implemented and now there are actual people involved. Whether they decide to give or not, there should always be a solid plan for following up with those you engaged.

One of the biggest complaints from potential donors or engaged patrons is that after an ask is made, there is nothing that comes after it. Donors, new and old, do not want to feel used or neglected once their usefulness has worn away. Development Directors or responsible staff should be at the ready to start following up with everyone the organization engaged within limits. And by limits, I mean, if they were engaged and live on the planet Earth, they deserve to be communicated with.

- What does "following-up" with donors look like?

Following up with donors will depend on scope and scale of the organization. The methodology may change but there are some basic tenets that need to be followed.

1. The first step in the following up process is communicating the organizations gratitude. From a commonsense point of view, saying thank you is generally a polite thing to say. However, it is the right to say and do. Donors and people in general want to be acknowledge for what they decided to give. The key-word in that last sentence was "decided." People make decisions on how, where and what to spend their resources on. This concept should not be lost on the organization of choice and from that perspective, following up to say thank you makes sense. Donors that are not thanked, typically do not give when asked again. The follow-up thank you can come in the form of handwritten letter,

email or phone call. For larger organizations with bigger budgets, you can even take a donor out to lunch for a more personalized touch. Again, find the medium that works best for your organization and do the follow up.

2. The second step after sending out the "thank you" notices, is to collect feedback. In this day and age, information is power. Gathering data for future campaigns is vital. A successful campaign breaks down what went right but also what went wrong. It is good to know the number of donors you have and the average size donation, however, it is even more pertinent to know what your donors liked or did not like about the engagement campaign. By attaching a short survey to an email, you are not only continuing the follow up process but you are creating investment in your donors. When asked the right questions, donors will feel as though they are a

part of the organizational processes and their input will be put to good use.

3. Finally, after the "thank you" notices have gone out and the data collected, the last step is to share the information and results with all staff and community. This sharing should premise allows all those involved to see what was accomplished. Additionally, it sheds a transparent light on the organization and continues open communication with the donors. A simple way to share this information with everyone is to add it to your existing website or send out an email. Depending on the size of the organization, the executive director can call for an all personnel meeting to go over the final results. This setting is also ideal to give out awards or certificates to staff that handled the heavy lifting.

- Who should do the follow up?

Typically, this task will fall on to the employees in the development department, if you are organization has one. If not, then whoever spearheaded the engagement campaign should be the first line of response for this area. They will have been the persons in charge of creating the contact list and setting the engagement strategy. However, tasks surrounding follow up can be doled out to interns or volunteers. Lastly, the blanket answer to who should do follow up is everyone! The entire organization has a responsibility to making sure donors and patrons are being recognized for their service and provision.

Key Questions Organizations Should Ask Themselves

1. Who inside your organization is responsible for follow-up?
2. What metrics are you using that demonstrate successful follow-up?

Recommendations for successful donor tracking

- Once a campaign or event is over, begin to reach out and communicate with donors and attendees.
- Invest in staff and software that helps with donor follow-up and tracking.
- Create an atmosphere within your organization that places donor follow-up as a priority to all staff.

Chapter 5: The Long View

Sustainability

The continued discussion among nonprofit leaders is how they can address engagement issues and attract more funding from their prospective communities. Information generated from research shows positive change in the local communities that nonprofits serve so that means you will need long-term funding. Nonprofits that are viable and have sustainability deliver high-impact services and resources.

Social environments and demographics of major cities are changing. As cities trend to attract and develop cultural melting pots, nonprofit organization leaders must look at the coinciding patterns. The donor makeup of these cities reflects the makeup of the community. For Americans, the data point to growth in educational attainment increases in financial capital and home ownership. This positive pattern can lead to assistance in communities via increased philanthropy and volunteerism. Targeting donors for engagement is a strategy that nonprofit development directors should undertake if they are looking toward the future of fundraising.

The traditional model of attempting to attract and retain donors is slowly changing, and nonprofit leaders must create newer pathways to draw funding. Nonprofit development directors are charged with attracting and cultivating donor bases for long-term sustainability. However, while nonprofit leaders understand the importance of fundraising they do not always know the best tactics for select groups and addressing disengagement.

Creating Sustainable Giving Efforts

Here are three approaches that can help guide a nonprofit organization to sustainability:

1. *Creating Awareness*

Organizations that develop memorable campaigns typically fair better in the long run. People remember what holds their attention and messaging that has a powerful voice means more giving.

2. *Dismantling silos and creating collaboratives*

The adage is true. There is strength in numbers. Organizations that have similar messages or similar donor related populations can begin to think about collaborating instead of competing. This level of partnership can assist with grant writing, resource sharing and agenda building.

3. *See things with a wider lens*

While some organizations do better to focus on one issue or symptom of the problem, at times it is better to expand your mission. By doing so, the organization can now be eligible for different types of grants, assistance or donations.

Organizations can become so focused on the fundamental business strategies, engagement and internal/external development that they quickly forget about sustainability. When developing a strategic plan or plan for engagement, it must have conversations around results and budget growth. The less reliant a nonprofit becomes on soft dollars [grants, endowed gifts, etc....], the more sustainable it becomes.

Social Responsibility and Sustainability

Philanthropy refers to the voluntary giving of resources that strategically affect nonprofit organizations. Current business trends indicate that individuals and companies are highly likely to give to communities in need or people at risk. The idea behind this premise is people in need are victims and need considerable help from those able to provide it.

Business leaders have begun the process of marrying traditional organizational ideals with philanthropy. Social responsibility or community philanthropy is the title bestowed on corporate charitable giving. Companies vary in size and scope, and size and scope typically determine the amount of giving done by a company. Racial makeup also plays a role in the amount and areas the funds affect.

Affected areas or persons are grouped into the stakeholder sphere of influence. Social responsibility is rooted in stakeholder theory, which is the reason the effect of philanthropy extends into different communities and causes. Individual donors have the influence of choice and make decisions based on their interests. Organizational leaders who look at fresh perspectives and partnerships can help remedy engagement issues.

Corporate philanthropy has grown over the years and helps mediate giving between personal interests and business. Company leaders use strategic philanthropy to locate specific areas of need and apply their collective resources toward those areas. By doing this consistently in a familiar environment, the premise is that the philanthropic effort will create a long-term effect (Salazar, Husted, & Biehl, 2012). The creation of this complementary relationship provides extended benefits and helps with sustainability.

Social responsibility also ties into understanding public awareness. Organizational leaders that express or exude confidence in the mission, vision, and values of the organization find greater sustainability. The perceived confidence relationship creates legitimacy and public awareness for donor campaigns. Volunteering is a segment of donor engagement. The call to service starts with motivation to help a nonprofit agency. The awareness of the donor creates positive experiences and promotes sustained engagement to the nonprofit organization.

Deeper connections can be made regarding social responsibility and corporate giving with ties to emotion-based giving and ethical business decisions. Donors become involved with companies they believe have the community's best interest at heart. Organizations affiliated with faith or spirituality tend to have an advantage with followers because their mission speaks to their personal beliefs. These kinds of connections are a motivator for giving, and nonprofit leaders that are not making the connection are not going to see donor engagement increase.

Donor Fatigue

Consistent asking for donations or funding from nonprofits can begin to weigh on the individuals always being asked. With so many nonprofits to choose one, there is bound to be an onslaught of solicitation on a continual basis. A major concern that nonprofit organizations should be on the lookout for is donor fatigue. This concept stems from nonprofit organizations making frequent calls to action and with a diminishing response rate.

While there is an emphasis placed on donor retention, the results of poorly managed engagement strategies contribute to donor fatigue. Development Directors cannot afford to lose donors and certainly do not want to lose them to other nonprofit organizations. Noticing and addressing donor fatigue should be at the top of the list for any nonprofit organization employee and creating intentional responses to address it are necessary. Here are some things to contribute to donor fatigue:

1. *Frequent invites to fundraising events*
    - Donors love hearing from you but do not always want to hear from you only when you want their money. Try hosting events that do not have a specific "ask."
2. *Inconsistent engagement over varied platforms*
    - Donors may or may not read the newsletter you send to the house but if that's all you send, it becomes stale. Documentation of all

the organization does plus spreading it out over several platforms creates engagement and visualization that things are happening with the donations.

3. *Being left out of the loop*
    - No one likes being told things after the fact. The same applies to your donor base. They have expectations to hear about organizational activities given they are donating money towards those goals. Again, communication is key and acknowledgement goes a long way.

Organizational leaders seeking to ward off donor fatigue must not only increase the quality of service provision but must also create real relationships with the communities they serve.

Key Questions Every Organization Should Ask About Sustainability

1. What strategic steps have you made to increase corporate donations?
2. What signs of donor fatigue can you spot with your organization?
3. What can your organization do to delivery varied forms of documentation?

Key Recommendations for Sustainability and Donor Fatigue

1. Maintain a healthy balance of "asks" and pure engagement. Donors want to hear about programs and activities, not just when you want donations.
2. Create deeper buy in from donors by making them committee members or hosts of the event. Donors that feel like ambassadors adopt a deeper investment and take on your cause to much greater lengths.
3. Use more visual and video-based aids for better impact with new and older donors. While stories

can be read, it is the presence of actually seeing the results play out via picture or video.

References

Salazar, J., Husted, B. W., & Biehl, M. (2012). Thoughts on the evaluation of corporate social performance through projects. *Journal of Business Ethics, 105,* 175-186. doi:10.1007/s10551-011-0957-z

Chapter 6: What's Next?

Wrapping It Up

Soliciting and asking for funds can be a very stressful experience for staff working at nonprofit organizations. However, that is easiest part. Once you have the ask down, it becomes more about donor management and sustained engagement. By creating a strong donor engagement plan, organizations can have a fluid roadmap to sustainability.

We must remember that all plans will not work for every organization. However, an organization must have a plan. Each person tasked with solicitation of funds and engagement should be involved in the plan creation and implementation. It will be during this phase that the organization can identify existing and new donor bases. Additionally, it will allow for ideation to come forth that can possibly highlight strengths or weaknesses in the current engagement model.

Donor engagement plans will change over time. You do not want a lot of time to pass without reassessing the current plan. Make sure to incorporate social media with engagement functions and continue to look for technological upgrades that can showcase a future forward giving campaign.

The start of any donor engagement campaign is not always easy. However, it can be done. It just takes the right information, the dedication and perseverance to do so. While competition for funds in any community is fierce, your organization can come out on top by staying connected to your community and understanding how they want to give.

Sample Call Sheet

Hello, [Contact Name]. I am [Callers Name] from [Organization Name]. How are you, this [morning or evening]?

(Around Holiday Seasons, starting with Happy New Year or Happy Holidays is acceptable.)

I would like to verify the information we have on file. Is it a good time to review your current contact information?"

Thank you for updating our files. When was the last time you donated money or time to [Organization Name]?"

We appreciate your prior donations more than you know. Would you be interested in donating this year?"

Your gift would help [Organization Name] to assist [Sample Demographic] in a big way. It is especially important this year."

Thank you for your donation, today. It means a lot to many people. [Organization Name] will benefit from your kindness."

Sample Donor Email

Dear Mack:

Thanks to you 2,349 men, women and children had a warm place to stay and a hot meal to eat this year. On behalf of them, thank you for saving their lives and their dignity.

I recently helped Crystal, a single mother of two children, move into a new apartment. She lived with her children at our shelter for 5 weeks. During that time she was able to get her children back into school, find a job, and save up for her first month's rent. Without your help, Crystal and her children would still be out on the street. Today, they are safe, warm and self-sufficient.

Every day, your support makes stories like Crystal's possible.

Today, we're launching our 2018 Year-End Campaign. Our goal is to help an additional 50 mothers, fathers, sons and daughters come in from the cold and find a way to get their lives back on track. You see, even though we helped over 2,300 people last year, there are still almost 1,000 homeless on our streets that we couldn't help, because we don't have the resources to do so.

That's why our goal for this campaign is to raise $40,000 by May 4th. If we raise that amount, we'll be able to provide food, shelter and clothing for 50 more people this year than last year. Joe, we need your help to make it happen.

Would you be willing to make a special year-end donation of $50, $100 or whatever you can afford to help us meet our goal and bring 50 more people in from the cold?

We simply can't do it without you. Your support will make a real, lasting impact in the lives of those who are still in need.

Please, click here to make your donation now. The lives of hundreds of others like Crystal are at stake.

Thank you for your continued support and friendship.

With gratitude,

Keith Cradle, PhD

Executive Director

The Cradle Shelter

P.S. Today, we launched our 2018 Year-End Campaign. Our goal is to raise $40,000 to help an additional 50 people get off the streets. We can't do it without your help. Will you make a gift of $25, $50 or whatever you can afford to help us meet this goal? Click here to make your donation now!

References

Aaker, J. V., & Mogilner, C. (2010). Nonprofits are seen as warm and for-profits as competent: Firm stereotypes matter. *Journal of Consumer, 37,* 224-237. doi:10.1086/651566

Bentley, J. (2014). Best practices in noncommercial radio fundraising: A practitioner perspective. *International Journal of Nonprofit and Voluntary Sector Marketing, 19,* 250-261. doi:10.1002/nvsm.1505

Boenigk, S., & Scherhag, C. (2014). Effects of donor priority strategy on relationship fundraising outcomes. *Nonprofit Management & Leadership, 24,* 307-336. doi:10.1002/nml.21092

Bortree, D., & Waters, R. (2014). Race and inclusion in volunteerism: Using communication theory to improve volunteer retention. *Journal of Public Relations*

Research, 26, 215-234. doi:10.1080/1062726X.2013.864245

Bucic, T., Harris, J., & Arli, D. (2012). Ethical consumers among the millennials: A cross national study. *Journal of Business Ethics, 110,* 113-131. Retrieved from https://www.jstor.org/journal/jbusiethi

Cacija, N. (2014). Preliminary empirical analysis of the relationship dynamics between marketing activities and fundraising success in nonprofit organizations. *Management Journal of Contemporary Management, 19,* 137-155. Retrieved from https://moj.efst.hr/management/

Calabrese, T., & Grizzle, C. (2012). Debt, donors, and the decision to give. *Journal of Pubic Budgeting, Accounting and Financial Management, 24,* 221-254. Retrieved from http://pracademics.com/index.php/jpbafm

Carter, V., & Marx, J. (2007). What motivates African-American charitable giving:

Findings from a national sample. *Administration in Social Work, 31*, 67-85.

doi:10.1300/J147v31n01_05

Chapleo, C. (2015). Brand "infrastructure" in nonprofit organizations: Challenges to successful brand building? *Journal of Marketing Communications, 21*, 199-209.

doi:10.1080/13527266.2012.741609

Cho, M., Schweickart, T., & Haase, A. (2014). Public engagement with nonprofit organizations on Facebook. *Public Relations Review, 40,* 565-567. doi:10.1016/j.pubrev.2014.01.008

Ford, J. B., & Merchant, A. (2010). Nostalgia drives donations: The power of charitable appeals based on emotions and intentions. *Journal of Advertising Research, 50,*

450. doi:10.2501/S0021849910091592

Gasman, M. (2010). A growing tradition? *Nonprofit Management and Leadership, 21,*

    121-138. doi:10.1002/nml.20016

Grizzle, C. (2015). Efficiency, stability and the decision to give to nonprofit arts and cultural organizations in the United States. *International Journal of Nonprofit and*

Voluntary Sector Marketing, 20, 226-237. doi:10.1002/nvsm.1521

Ihm, J. (2015). Network measures to evaluate stakeholder engagement with nonprofit organizations on social networking sites. *Public Relations Review, 41,* 501-503.

    doi:10.1016/j.pubrev.2015.06.018

Ilicic, J., & Baxter, S. (2014). Fit in celebrity-charity alliances: When perceived celanthropy benefits nonprofit organisations. *International Journal of*

Nonprofit and Voluntary Sector Marketing, 16, 200-208. doi:10.1002/nvsm.1497

Jackson, T. (2001). Young African Americans: A new generation of giving behavior. *International Journal of Nonprofit and Voluntary Sector Marketing, 6,* 243-253.

Khodakarami, F., Petersen, J., & Venkatesan, R. (2015). Developing donor relationships: The role of the breadth of giving. *Journal of Marketing, 79,* 77-93. doi:10.1509/jm.14.0351

Kim, Y., & Lee, W. (2014). Networking for philanthropy: Increasing volunteer behavior via social networking sites. *Cyberpsychology, Behavior, and Social Networking, 17*(3), 160-165. doi:10.1089/cyber.2012.0415

Kirk, K., Abrahams, A., & Ractham, P. (2016). E-progression of nonprofit organization websites: US versus Thai charities. *Journal of Computer Information Systems, 56,*

244-252. doi:10.1080.08874417.2016.153918

Ko, Y. J., Gibson, H., & Kim, M. (2011). Understanding donors: A case of university performing arts programs in the USA. *International Journal of Nonprofit and Voluntary Sector Marketing, 16*, 166-182. doi:10.1002/nvsm.411

Lovejoy, K., Waters, R., & Saxton, G. (2012). Engaging stakeholders through Twitter: How nonprofit organizations are getting more out of 140 characters or less. *Public Relations Review, 38*, 313-318. doi:10.1016/j.pubrev.2012.01.005

Malhotra, N., & Smith, A. (2011). Social and tax implications of planned giving. *Journal of Applied Business Research, 27*, 39-43. doi:10.19030/jabr.v27i6.6464

Mataira, P., Morelli, P., Matsuoka, J., & Uehara-McDonald, S. (2014). Shifting the paradigm: New directions for non-profits and funders in an era of diminishing resources. *Social Business, 4*, 231-244. doi:10.1362/204440814X14103454934212

Mano, R. (2014). Social media, social causes, giving behavior and money contributions. *Computers in Human Behavior, 31,* 278-293. doi:10.1016/j.chb.2013.10.044

McKeever, B. (2013). From awareness to advocacy: Understanding nonprofit communication, participation, and support. *Journal of Public Relations Research, 25*, 307-328. doi:10.1080/1062726X.2013.806868

McMurray, A., Islam, M., Sarros, J., & Pirola-Merlo, A. (2013). Workplace innovation in a nonprofit organization. *Nonprofit Management & Leadership, 23*, 367-388. doi:10.1002/nml.21066

Millar, P., & Doherty, A. (2016). Capacity building in nonprofit sport organizations:

Development of a process model. *Sport Management Review, 19,* 365-377. doi:10.1016/j.smr.2016.01.002

Mottino, F., & Miller, E. (2005). Philanthropy among African American donors in the New York metropolitan region: A generational analysis. *New Directions for Philanthropic Fundraising, 48,* 31-46. Retrieved from https://www.researchgate.net/journal/1542-7846_New_Directions_for_Philanthropic_Fundraising

Paulin, M., Ferguson, R., Schattke, K., & Jost, N. (2014). Millennials, social media, prosocial emotions, and charitable causes: The paradox of gender differences. *Journal of Nonprofit & Public Sector Marketing, 26,* 335-353. doi:10.1080/104955142.2014.965069

Paulin, M., Ferguson, R., Jost, N., & Fallu, J. (2014). Motivating millennials to engage in charitable causes through social media. *Journal of Service Management, 25*, 334-348. doi:10.1108/JOSM-05-2013-0122

Powers, E., & Yaros, R. (2012). Cultivating support for nonprofit news organizations: Commitment, trust, and donating audiences. *Journal of Communication Management, 17*, 157-170. doi:10.1108/13632541311318756

Samuel, O., Wolf, P., & Schilling, A. (2013). Corporate volunteering: Benefits and challenges for nonprofits. *Nonprofit Management & Leadership, 24*, 163-179. doi:10.1002/nml.21089

Scherhag, C., & Boenigk, S. (2013). Different or equal treatment? Donor priority strategy and fundraising performance assessed by a propensity score matching study. *Nonprofit Management & Leadership, 23*, 443-472. doi:10.1002/nml.21074

Schloderer, M., Sarstedt, M., & Ringle, C. (2014). The relevance of reputation in the nonprofit sector: The moderating effect of socio-demographic characteristics. *International Journal of Nonprofit and Voluntary Sector Marketing, 19,* 110-126. doi:10.1002/nvsm.1491

Schneider, J. (2003). Small, minority-based nonprofits in the information age. *Nonprofit Management & Leadership, 13,* 385-399. doi:10.1002/nml.6

Smith, S., Windmeijer, F., & Wright, E. (2013). Peer effects in charitable giving: Evidence from the (running) field. *Economic Journal, 125,* 1053-1071. doi:10.1111/ecoj.12114

Smitko, K. (2012). Donor engagement through twitter. *Public Relations Review, 38,* 633-635. doi:10.1016/j.pubrev.2012.05.012

Swanson, L. (2013). A strategic framework for nonprofits. *Nonprofit Management &*

Leadership, 23, 303-323. doi:10.1002/nml.21067

Wang, C., Duan, Z., & Yu, L. (2016). From nonprofit organization to social enterprise. *International Journal of Contemporary Hospitality Management, 28*, 1287-1306.

doi:10.1108/IJCHM-05-2014-0230

Waniak-Michalak, H., & Zarzycka, E. (2015). Financial and non-financial factors motivating individual donors to support public benefit organizations.

Comparative Economic Research, 18, 131-152. doi:10.1515/cer-2015-0008

Van Slyke, D., Ashley, S., & Johnson, J. (2007). Nonprofit performance, fund-raising effectiveness, and strategies for engaging African Americans in philanthropy.

American Review of Public Administration, 37, 278-305.

doi:10.1177/0275074006294390

Zhu, W., & Cheung, M. (2014). Multiple relationship-management roles among communicators in not-for-profit organizations. *Human Service Organizations: Management, Leadership & Governance, 38,* 423-434.

doi:10.1080/23303131.2014.943918

www.ingramcontent.com/pod-product-compliance
Lightning Source LLC
Chambersburg PA
CBHW070956240526
45469CB00016B/1205